THE POWER OF KNOWING AND LOVING YOURSELF

STANITRA ROBINSON

Copyright © 2021 by Stanitra Robinson

THE POWER OF KOWING AND LOVING YOURELF

All rights reserved. No part of this publication may be reproduced, distributed, or transmitted in any form or by any means, including photocopying, recording, or other electronic or mechanical methods, without the prior written permission of the publisher, except in the case of brief quotations embodied in critical reviews and certain other noncommercial uses permitted by copyright law. For permission requests, write to the publisher, addressed "Attention: Permissions Coordinator," at info@beyondpublishing.net

Quantity sales special discounts are available on quantity purchases by corporations, associations, and others. For details, contact the publisher at the address above.

Orders by U.S. trade bookstores and wholesalers. Email info@ BeyondPublishing.net

Th e Beyond Publishing Speakers Bureau can bring authors to your live event. For more information or to book an event contact the Beyond Publishing Speakers Bureau speak@BeyondPublishing.net

Th e Author can be reached directly at BeyondPublishing.net

Manufactured and printed in the United States of America distributed globally by BeyondPublishing.net

New York | Los Angeles | London | Sydney

ISBN Hardcover: 978-1-637920-37-4

*I dedicate this book to my family,
my mom, Jina Robinson, and my dad, Solomon Robinson.
I love you guys. Without you, I would not have life,
and I thank God every day for you.*

This book has empty pages, so you can follow along and write things down to help you along your journey with God and to be happy and free. These are some of the things I did to help myself. I pray this will help you learn how to soar and not get poisoned by hanging with the wrong crowd.

I hope this message will bless you and help you, stay away fear,

for God hath not given you a spirit of fear. Fear does not come from God, fear comes from Satan. It is one of his weapons to stagnate and stunt your purpose. Fear is a paralytic weapon that the enemy uses to slow you down from pursuing your purpose. God wants you to move forward in your purpose, plan, and destiny. God has not given you a spirit of fear, for we walk by faith and not by sight.

I am writing this book to help you gain the trust that God has for you and that His love is unconditional. I have felt God's love, and I pray that you will feel it, too, by not fearing, but growing and glowing as you need to. ENJOY yourself and remember, do not be afraid to share your story—it may be ugly, but it could save a life. Just look at yourself and look up and be happy with what you have become. You are reading this book and you are going through the steps that helped me. I pray this will help you repent and turn to God, He will make it beautiful.

MY LIFE

It all started when I was a kid, I was active and happy, and I was always flipping in the house. In my first book, Speaking Your Way to Success, I talk about loving life and how life is crazy, but that it is up to you on how you want to do things and change. My childhood was a breeze. I forgot some things, but I remember my sister telling me that my parents would fight and she would cover my ears, so I did not hear them. I was only three years old, so I was thankful to have not really remembered what happened. I was always sheltered by my sister, and I thank God she did. As I got older, I liked to live life on the edge. I love camping, skydiving, and bungee jumping. I have friends who own a bridge. It is in Battle Ground, Washington, not far from Portland, Oregon, where I was raised. It's bungee.com—it is so cool. If you want to get over your fear of heights, I highly recommend them. Now that I am closer to Six Flags, I go there to de-stress and have fun. I know we always say I will try to get over my fear or I will try something new, and there is nothing wrong with trying, but try to have a mindset saying that I will. If you try something, and try and try, you will end up failing, so have the mindset to do it and stay consistent and believe in yourself and tell yourself you can do it. Now, I am looking for a higher thrill.

When I was a kid, I had so many animals: a bird, named Agauns, a bunny, named Sugar, and of course, Saddie, a metal pull toy with big red wheels—his tail was a spring that moved back and forth; he was a squirrel. I always loved animals, and as I was growing up in Seattle, we always had animals. When we moved to Portland, Oregon, we had them also. We moved to Oregon when I was about three years old, and when we arrived in Portland, my mom and dad were always at a job, and I was with my older sister. Fast forward to the age of 13: I was in gymnastics and basketball, just loving life. I was a gymnast for a while, then fast forward to high school. I was drinking, partying, and smoking cigarettes, and what I called it at the time was having fun—yes, having so much fun.

I was in my own apartment by the age of 21, drinking, partying, and smoking weed. I fell down a flight of stairs concerted stairs and broke my leg drunk. I remember I had a new car and tried to start it while I was drunk. My neighbor was looking out for me and asked where I was going; I told her I wanted to make sure it started. I am so happy she was there. Now, I look down and see my ankle and my scar and realize that God was with me.

My family did not go to church at all, and I was never brought up like that. Anything bad that has happened to you in life, embrace it. That is part of your story and growth with God. I got a job at Chuck E. Cheese, my first job out of high school. I graduated with a 3.5 GPA, and they had me on a modified diploma. There were some things that I wanted to do, and the school and they said no. I wanted to be in science, and they said I was a low level. I wish I could go back and do harder classes. You see, we need to run with people who are successful in life. Unfortunately, I was still young. They did have me setup with a work program so that was fun I worked at borders book store than chuck e cheese I did not know anything about business but I meet some amazing people on my journey TY and ANN Rustrum and Michelle and Aaron Ketchem and little did i know they taught me more than ever on how to start your own business through amway and I was blessed but to get back to my younger years before I started amway

When I finally settled down, I found a boyfriend who was so cool. Matt was into music and doing different shows on stage. I stayed with this guy for two years. I moved in with him and really started my life with him. I helped him, and I was growing closer to him. As he took off and started making money, he decided that his rapping was better than me. As time went on, I forgave him. I left and went back to my mom's house. I lived with her and helped with the family business. I took care of people with disabilities and more. It was an in-home care through the State of Oregon. I decided that was not for me and got my own place.

I started working at different jobs, and I came across Fred Meyer. I only worked there for two years; it was a grocery store, kind of like a Walmart. I cleaned floors and waxed them, but then they found a different company and pulled us away. I was making good money, but they decided to let us go or rehire for no benefits at all; I had full benefits. Then, I found Safeway, another grocery store and got on there. I was there for seven years, then, I was let go. I decided to go back to my mom and help her out with the family business. As I was working at Safeway, they hired this girl named Autumn, and we became good friends. She invited me to church, and I was baptized after six months of going. I invited my family and friends. Autumn, my coaches from amway were there, and her dad were the only people who showed up. It was so good to know there were people that were so amazing and made me feel so good after I broke my leg I now realised that God was with me. She moved from California, and her mom was still in California. She moved from California for Safeway, a job. As we were both let go, her and her mom found a place in Texas. Me and her lived together at the time. We were struggling to pay bills, but we had a cute cookie cutter home. It was expensive; she invited me to live with her and her mom in Texas. So, I decided to move with her. I was so scared leaving my home, I had everything together, my mom was helping me with my new truck, and now I was leaving that all behind. As I was moving forward, pulling the U-Haul, I was thinking, I need to go back. What was I doing but God kept me going? My mom was paying for everything, but I was independent and did not want that for myself.

I was saying I loved animals and being adventurous. I got my bearded dragon in 2008. He was at PetSmart, and I had no idea about him. So, I did my reading at the library, and I was into it so much. I got into reading about snakes and more lizards. Then, I realized that I wanted him, so I got him. It was pretty easy, because I had snakes. Also, so as I am driving to Texas in my truck looking at him, something told me to keep moving thank GOD, that there is something better for you. I knew it was God. Even though I was scared, I pushed forward, and as I looked at Zafari, my animal, I knew this would be good for him. It is warmer in Texas than Oregon.

When I got to Texas, I did not know anyone. It took me two weeks to find a job, and I was already late on my truck payments, but that did not stop me. Within two months, I moved out of Autumn's mom's house and still had my truck. I was driving around and saw this cool pet store, Polly's, in Universal City. I talked to the guy who worked there, and they had a huge snake there. He had some problems; they did everything they could for him. He was pretty expensive, but they gave him to me for cheaper price. I was so thankful to get him, I love that pet store to this day. I found my own place with a new job at the HEB warehouse as a machine operator. They had the same machines at Safeway, so I was hired quick. My truck had gone back; the bank picked it up. I got a new car, but before that, I just biked back and forth. I was very thankful some of the people there gave me rides home. Even though we go through things, we grow through them and keep positive. Even though it may get hard to look up and thank God and His sacrifices He made to give us life, no complaints. Sometimes, we complain and forget, but do not do that; look up and smile. I guarantee you will feel good. I now wake up and before I open my eyes, I drop to my knees and pray. At the end of my book, I will talk about how I give my feet, my eyes, and my soul to God every morning. You can hang that up in your bathroom, just keep reading, you will see it. It is the dedication of life to Christ.

For two months, I was not driving, but I had met some amazing people. Before my truck was repossessed, I meet Krystal and Cloud. Krystal, my coworker's wife, has helped me a lot. She is a wonderful mom to an autistic child, who is doing so well. It doesn't seem like he has a disability and Cloud, a solar panel expert, will cut your energy bill in half or to nothing.

When I moved into my own place, I was talking about driving around. I came across this market, and it was huge. Lots of different shops, and since I had Zafari with me, everyone stopped. One girl stopped me, Erica. She said, "Oh, a bearded dragon—he's a little older." I told her, "Yes, he is," and she said, "Have you ever heard of Alamo City Reptile Rescue? I said, "No, I just moved here from Portland, Oregon." She asked why, so I told her to start new and fresh. She said, "Wow, cool," and she added me on her Facebook. She also added this reptile rescue group.

When my truck was picked up, I had no way to feed Zacara, my blood python I got from Polly's, so I got on the reptile group and asked about a rat to help. I only had two animals when I moved into my new place. I got help from a girl who brought a rat to me, Darianna. We talked, and we became friends. After we were friends, I moved in with her, and we became roommates. After living with her for two years, she moved to Tennessee with her boyfriend, and she got a house with him. I am very thankful for her, as she taught me more about snakes. We had a zoo there at our apartment, but everything was taken care of. It was so nice to see all the reptiles that we had. I would even take some of her snakes to different birthday parties and events, even though I did not have my license or LLC (limited liability company). It was a blessing to see the kids have fun. We all have to start somewhere in life. A job is not something that will be there forever, but there is nothing wrong with starting your own company. It may be hard, but if you have what it takes, find something you have a passion for and go with it. God will give you the supernatural power to keep moving forward.

Alamo City Reptile Rescue was on Facebook. They grew so much that they moved into PetSmart. Doing different education and adoptions after helping and volunteering my time with them, I met up with Homies with Scales and started volunteering with them. It was so fun. When I moved into my new place, I had my car and was able to get around, I volunteered more. I was doing adoption events in PetSmart and at Artic Ape, for a reptile fun event for the kids. Artic Ape is a good ice cream shop. It is cool when you go in. It has a cool set up, and it just took off from there. I was seeing these kids have so much fun; it made my heart happy. I did an event for my apartments, and the kids there had fun.

After COVID-19 hit, I thought, Well, I paid off my car, and I am getting Texas Proud pay, so I decided to start Springing Scales. I bring the reptile adventure to you, and since then, I've written a chapter in a book, which made me an international, bestselling author. The book sold and hit #1 on Amazon, and I've helped small businesses with my reptiles. I've gotten people over their fears of snakes, and as I was on stage, I got Derrick Hill over his fear of snakes. He's also writing a book called The Marble Effect. His chapter title in Speaking Your Way to Success is called, "A Speakers Destiny Calling".

God has put some amazing people in my life. My biggest wish is to meet Steve Harvey and put Zacara around him hahaha. Also, to get more information out there, so people know that these animals are not as bad as you think. I also want to go see Ellen DeGeneres or Wendy Williams—my sister and I watched her. I have started something so amazing with these animals, and I am leaning more as I go. God has a plan for me; I keep praying and loving myself as much as I love God and my animals. The reptile care is not as bad as you think it is; my heart is so happy I get to do this. I have to do this sometimes; we wake up and say, "Ugh, I have to go to work," or "I have to run errands"—no, no, no, change your mindset and say, "I get to do this, I get to go to work, and I get to start my own business." I get to do these things that we complain about; we need to be happy and once again look up and smile. There are people that have to get up, go get water, boil it, and take a small bath river water that they have to bathe in and drink. They have to get water for their family; it's a couple of trips, so be happy we are so blessed to jump into a shower and have running water, or jump into a car and go to the store.

This is the part of the book where you tell yourself you have value. Helping yourself be stronger than ever. I will go into the care of the animals first, then the power of believing in yourself and knowing how to be one with yourself. The power of caring and self-love, just remember we serve a good God, He loves you, and now it's time you love yourself.

The Power of Knowing Reptiles and Their Care

I am just getting started. I want to be able to quit HEB and start helping more with these animals i am blessed to have the job to fund the business. I have adopted some animals from the rescue that no one else could really take on. I have a leopard gecko that has two broken hands and a bearded dragon with MBD, which is metabolic bone disease, which they can get from no care. She had the heat lamp, but she did not have the sun rays they need to help their bones. The sun's rays help her with her scales and her digestion. It's hard for them to be comfortable without the sun; they need it, so the spine will be healthy and not brittle. It's sad, but I am so happy God has blessed me with these animals.

I have a Tegu argentine black and white; she was in a 55-gallon tote eating Alpo dog food—they can have a little dog food, but not Alpo. They mostly eat eggs with the shell for extra calcium, raw chicken hearts, or raw chicken livers. I have had people call me about their bearded dragons not eating and could it be the temperature outside? I always tell people that if your house is at a good temperature—at least 85 degrees—snakes don't need a heating pad.

Now with bearded dragons, they need basking, UVA and UVB lights, if they don't have that or calcium, they can develop MBD or worse. Never think that a breaded dragon needs a friend; they see you as their friend. That's just the basic care for a bearded dragon. They can be taken out of their cage to let them get sun. They will not get the sun rays if you have their cage next to a window; it's warm, but it will not do anything for them.

Snakes are easy: you can put them in a tote and put holes in it. Use Eco Earth; it's a coconut substrate, and if they eat it, it's okay. Make sure you put the heat outside—not inside—the tank, to make sure they have a hot and cold side. Do not use heating rocks for your snakes; that is a good way to burn them. The heating rocks look cool, but if you use them, use them on a bearded dragon. Cut the cord to the heating rock; they can still put off heat while the rock is in the cage under the light. Mites are a little bug that will live right at the base of your snake's chin; they are like fleas on a dog, but they are on a snake. Mites are black and hard to get rid of, but if you use Dawn and unrefined organic coconut oil, you can pull them out of their scales, and they will suffocate. You can also use coconut oil for dry and rough scales on a snake; you can use it on a dragon, but just a little if they are having trouble shedding.

The Power of Saying I can, and I Will

I am so happy to have met some amazing people, and I have pushed myself out of an employee mindset into an entrepreneur mindset. It was not easy, but it's well worth it. An employee mindset is when you are told what you are worth and your work. They are helping their business grow as they tell you what to do, nothing wrong with it because this is how we are taught. When we are born, our parents are used to it, because they were taught like this. Teaching us that having a job and getting good grades is what we need to do, because that is their JOB. JUST OVER BROKE, TY told me that hahaha.i have ran with that ever since i meet him through AMWAY this is where i stared to grow within God and know a little about business and growing people where always making fun of me about staring amway but i did not let that stop me

You can change your mindset, but you must be willing to change. It is the power of changing your mindset, to grow, sometimes we have to go through things, but we grow through them. I have found happiness in my job today; it's helping with bills and funding my business. If you look at time at a job, you are putting money away in a 401(k), and as you are, you are working so hard to retire at the age of 65 years old, and some people think that's okay and having vacation only four times a year. I encourage you to find your purpose and keep your job, but find something on the side you like. Love for me, is the animals and helping them and seeing people smile and getting over their fears. I believe a 401(k) is 40 years of your life and 1k a month, there is nothing wrong with this, but if you look at the odds, it's better to build yourself up and don't let anybody say you can't, or you a dumb and if they do, then prove them wrong. Keep on pushing, forgive them, and come back in love, instead of hate.

This is why I started my own business. I have had so many jobs, and they don't care: you will be replaced. Schools teach us how to get a good job, and as I say, there is nothing wrong with that, but do you really think they know how to build a successful business? Surround yourself with like-minded people, who are making good money and have the things you want. It's not about being materialistic, but your mindset will be strong, just keep it up. Find someone you can consider working with. Make sure they are successful and get into their programs, like Daniel Gomez. Make sure they believe in what you believe in, like Daniel Gomez, he is close to God and the way he prays is amazing. Most of all, believe in yourself.

The Power of Not Being Worried

We do this all the time; we worry about things we can't control and things we can control. We have to think positive, even if it's a negative situation. Don't get caught up in a worry, God made the ultimate sacrifice for us. Just remember you got this and pray and believe in yourself. Don't worry, I feel like worry can be a part of a fear. Don't let that happen, choose not to let the spirt of heaviness weigh you down. Choose to surrender to God, let Christ lift every burden. Choose to worship God, don't worship the weight or bondage of the past. Choose to redirect your focus and worship Christ. When you begin to focus on and magnify the cares and worries of the world, they will begin to weigh you down. When you chose to focus on your worries, cares, and anxieties, they will begin to overload you. Don't let the cares of this world grip and lord over your heart or spirit. Choose to focus on God and not the weight of the world. Proverbs 12:25 NLT declares worry

The Power of Eating Well and Clean

I have a second business, TLC: Total Life Changes. It's a total life change; they have products that detox, and you can take this detox. It has vitamins and all the good things you need to detox; totallifechanges.com/35099993 is my website. It's the power of detoxification to your mind, health, body, and spirit. I like to detox my body and mind with nothing but positivity and loving myself. Sugar will spike you up and crash you later. The powers of eating clean will help you stay in the right mind. When I was eating bad, my bad ankle would swell. I could not figure it out; once I got rid of the sugar and started eating better and working out, I saw a huge difference. The headache stopped and the swelling went down; it will help your skin also.

I found this place called Empower Nutrition through Herbalife. They have workouts, and I started going. They are amazing; her and her mom have their own shop off of Perrin Bital. They have helped me grow. Michelle, the mom, and her daughter, Danielle, have kicked my butt in the workouts. Tru Fit has been amazing. I do different events with the animals at Tru Fit. I've gotten people over their fears of snakes at that gym. It has been amazing. Just stay focused, and remember: consistency is key. With God, you will be good to take care of yourself. Your body is God's temple; take care of it as much as He takes care of us.

The Power of Sin, Don't Let it Get to You or Get You Down

Sure, we have all sinned. I found myself sleeping around trying to find love and pleasing myself with toys and feeling empty inside. I felt so bad when I got up; I just cried. I ended up going into a dark place and started feeling horrible about myself, feeling nasty and disgusting. So, I tried to please myself with toys and sex, but when I went to God and prayed and gave it to Him, I called the guys I was sleeping with and told them, "I am sorry, but I have prayed, and God told me, 'I love you, you do not need this.'" I told the guys that, and they said, "What? Whatever. Can I come over?" I said, "Sorry, no. I can't do this anymore. God loves me, I have to forgive myself. God loves you and me, and I am not of the world." I have the higher power to say no, and God is telling me I have been sleeping by myself now. God has put the right people in my life to help me though. Sin, I know this is a lot of information, but God put this in my heart to share with you. I did not want to say anything about this, but this is part of my story, and I am not holding anything back. If God told me, then I must obey. He loves me, and once I gave him my yes and my obedience, I woke up unstoppable. You can do the same. God died for our sins, and one person may be going through a rough time; that's when you get on your knees and pray. Let the Holy Spirit heal your heart, and if you need anything, come to my church in San Antonio, Texas. Xtreme Harvest Church, 7015 Wurzbach Road, or you can email me. I love you, and you got this, believe and forgive.

The Power of Loving Yourself

We all have special powers. We can use them for what we love to do, build something, and give it all to God. That is what I did. I believe with God, all things are possible. The love of faith is very powerful; no one can take that away from you. The only person who can take that away is you. Daniel Gomez, my friend, a coach, and an amazing person, told me I was born to fly. He also said, "Your best is yet to come."

I got to meet him at a (TLC) Total Life Changes weight loss event. It's a detox tea that I sell; it has everything you need to detox your body. His wife, Mari Gomez is a cancer survivor. They have changed my life. I told him I wanted to speak, and he said, "Yeah, okay," and kind of blew me off, but I was determined. So, I spoke and blew everyone away. He even said on stage that he did had not taken me seriously, but he worked with me, and I believed in myself and ran with it.

As I was at work, I was thinking, "How can I help?" So, I started my own business with the reptiles. Then, I was thought, Let me start with my name, so I took myself back to grade school, where they had you put your name down and you see good things about yourself, like S_T_A_N_I_T_R_A, so the S=smart T=talented A=athletic N=never stops I=intelligent T=truthful R=rambunctious A=authentic. Put that on your mirror, so when you get up, you can see yourself at the end. You want to write most of all, "I am a child of God, and I am happy." Always put in your mind that today will be a good day, no matter what. Keep going and growing and glowing; there is nothing wrong with mess-ups or friends who may keep us down. We forgive and never forget, but we always bless them and pray for them. See forgiveness is for you, not for them, if they take it, well then, great. Always forgive and pray for them and keep them in your heart. Always care and respect; keep that hate away.

The Power of Being Faithful to God and Our Family

I feel like since we work so much at a JOB—Just Over Broke—job, I feel like we don't spend time with God, because our work will not allow it, or we make excuses to not spend time with God. God wants us to spend time with him every morning, for us to wake with just a simple thank you. God took the ultimate sacrifice. When we come to God, talk to Him, let Him forgive you, and it will make you feel better. Be true to your heart, forgive, and repent, and you will see his faithfulness and love. May our hearts be fully faithful and fully committed to the Lord, our God, to live by His decrees and obey his commands as at this time. 1 Kings 8:61 NIV

The Power of the Holy Spirit

The Holy Spirit is real. He lives in all of us. You need to receive it with an open heart and an open mind. We may think He's not real, but let me tell you something: HE'S REAL! It's such a beautiful thing. I can't explain or express how much love and affection I felt when I felt him touch my heart. I sleep so well, and when I wake up, I smile and say, "Thank you Jesus for Him." For you, the Holy Spirit saves and heals. Almighty God, thanks for healing me and saving me. Only You have the power to change me. Now, I can go and heal other people. Thanks for giving me all of you; now, I want to give you all of me. Think and live like that, and you will feel so much better. Souls and lives are changed by His love, the power of the Holy Spirit. Picture yourself living your life better than ever. Picture yourself not in pain anymore. Picture yourself feeling blessed and loved every day. Our body is not equipped to handle the power of the Holy Spirit, but when you get a little bit of Him, it's life-changing. The thing I want you to really focus on is the gift God has for us. His spirit and speaking in tongues, I will give you some Bible verses.

The Power of Speaking in Tongues and Our Gift from God, the Holy Spirit

1-John chapter 3 verses 1 through 8.

2-Mark chapter 16 verses 15-17. If you read most of this, it will say, "And these signs will accompany those who believe in my name, they will drive out demons, they will speak in new tongues." Verse 18 in Mark says, "They will pick up snakes with their hands, and when they drink deadly poison, it will not hurt them at all. They will lay their hands on sick people, and they will become well." When I read this, I was shocked; this is what I do to help reptiles. I don't drink the venom, but I do take the hurt away from them. Also, if you look in Acts, chapter 1 versese 3-9 and 8-12; this all talks about how we speak in tongues to speak to God. It is a beautiful thing to God, and He understands us. That is how we communicate. Look at Luke chapter 11 verse 13 and repeatedly say, "Thank you, Jesus." Let God take over your mouth and let God handle your stirring. Let yourself go, in Jesus' name. Now, speak and say it from your heart, "Thank you, Jesus, thank you, Jesus, thank you, Jesus." Keep saying it, "Thank you, Jesus."

The Power that Satan Does Not Have Over You, God Has the Power

Satan—yes, I said it— Satan has power, but that's up to you. If you want to believe the lies, start trusting in God, and you will see the lies that Satan will put in front of you to make you hurt or manipulate you. If you feel good about something and it's easy to get and you cry about it because you can't explain how you got it, that's God, helping you. When I got my new car, there was no way a company I've owed would finance me. I've had bad credit, a repo, and I got my ex-boyfriend a car, and two days later, he totaled it. That is on my credit, but praise God, Satan will make things hard for you, but God will clear it all up for you. I forgave my ex-boyfriend and won with God. God is good; Satan is a scammer and a lie. We have to be prepared to be hit by Satan. satan kept me in the dark about sleeping around and made me feel bad about evertying and once i parayed and gave it to God i was unstopable and forgave myself

I was looking up Satan and how he works, and it brought me to a satanic website that was into bad things. There were naked women around, and the guy was so happy with his horns, and I deleted it really quick. Sometimes, we see this and want to read more, because people look for the negative things to read, but as we grow and keep growing closer with God, remember He sees everything. We have to be strong to please God, and yes, Satan watches us also, but God will give us the power to shut hell up and move forward. Just stay strong, and God will give His power and strength to us. Look at the Bible: God is always righteous, and He has the upper hand. When I came to God, I was teaching myself about the Bible. Some of it I understood, but some was deep, and I cried. I was able to stop cussing; it was a curse coming out of my mouth, and I was into self-pleasure. I threw away my habits and went to the altar and cried so hard. I slept well that night. Don't let Satan win; let God take you. When i was groing up i mentoind i did not know God but i am so blessed that God knows me and he saw me and loves me for me and now i can worship and give him my whole heart

PRAY THIS

Heavenly Father, Satan has been like a roaring lion in my life, roaring lies into my soul. I want to take each one to you and ask you if these are truths or lies, and in the name of Jesus, I reject the lies of Satan. This work he has done in my heart, I accept your truths and the work Jesus did for me at Calvary. I choose to turn those thoughts over to Him and accept new, truthful descriptions about myself. Thank you for taking away these lies. In Jesus' name, AMEN.

The Power of Self-Love

Self-love is something we don't do. We make excuses, or we make negative thoughts for ourselves. Every negative thought has positivity behind it. You need to run for the positive. I always take a negative situation and turn it around into a positive, so that way, you can make it through your day without being angry. Just tell yourself, "You got this."

There is a guy on Facebook, his name is Dahar Mann, and he is a producer for his studio. He makes these little skits that are amazing, and he's always giving $100 away after his new videos. You have to share it to win. He is really good and changing lives just by what he says. It's really good for your mind to change the way you see negative situations; you will start to look for more positives.

If you look up self-love, it says that it means having a high regard for your own well-being and happiness. Self-love means taking care of your own needs and not sacrificing your well-being to please others. Self-love means not settling for less than you deserve. I have followed this and loved this as much as I love myself. It's not hard to love yourself, and don't think of it as selfish. The definition of selfish says, "of a person, action, or motive lacking consideration for others, concerned chiefly with one's own personal profit or pleasure". It does not say anything about yourself, so please take care of yourself. I dare you; I double dare you; it may just make you happy and smile. Just like Daniel says, "You were born to fly, you were made for greatness." Take time to know yourself and know what you what in life and love. Take time to forgive and help others, even if they did you wrong… you never know, they can be a huge blessing in your life. Please look up Daniel Gomez, You Were Born to Fly. I read this book, and he can help. He also has amazing programs that can help you. There is Daniel Hill, Undefeated, Broken Into Purpose, Joy Brown. I've met all of these people and many more. Find yourself with God and one of these books, and you will catch the Holy Ghost. He will bring you to your knees, and you will cry. Find some good music: "Great Are You Lord", by Casting Crowns on YouTube and here is my heat lord by casting crowns i worship to theses songs.

The Power of Positive Thinking

What is positive thinking, you ask? Positive thinking is a mental and emotional attitude of expecting good and favorable results, and not getting discouraged when plans do not proceed as expected. It means trying over again and not accepting defeat. It's an attitude of focusing on the good and positive in a situation—and not on the negative. With this mindset, you will not accept defeat; you will not allow anything or anyone negative to affect your mood or state of mind. Boom, baby.

This is how I have been living, and let me tell you: I got my bike stolen, and all I could think about is, What if a loved one was passing, and someone needed to get somewhere fast and they saw my bike as an opportunity to get there fast? I looked up and said, "Thank you, Jesus," and smiled. I said to myself, I have a car, and then, I just went on my day without being mad. If you don't like someone, start looking for things you do like about them; stop looking for the negative. Forgiving people and forgiving yourself is hard, but once you do it, I promise it will get easy. Change is never easy, but you can, and you will speak it into existence.

The Power of Leading the Power of Adding Value to Yourself

Learning and being valuable, seeing yourself as a value, take action, and be consistent. Consistence is key, learn more value in yourself, see the value of yourself. The job you have may not have this, yes, they see the value in you, but they pay you what they think you are worth. It's time to see the value in yourself and see the real value in yourself. Remember run, spring forward, and don't go back. We are never taught to lead; we are taught to follow. Going to school, I remember when I wanted to do science and math, and they told me I could not, because of my low scores. Then, when I went to ABE—adult basic education—in school, I wanted to get into a good class for science and that was college when I took the class.

Let me tell you: when I found value in myself, Daniel was there for me. I have paid a lot of money, less than what I was going to pay for school. Michael D. Butler, my publisher, has been amazing. He has helped me with my book I have written, Speak Your Way to Success, and now this one. Find people who find value in you, but really believe in yourself. It is all mindset. Give your fears to God and let yourself soar. Think about fourth grade: we were all in line, following each other. That was a way to get us trained, but follow God, and you will see things change in your heart.

The Power of Not Fearing

Fear will hurt us, fear will kill us, it can make you suffocate, and your immune system can shut down. It says on google that the human body and fear weakens our immune system; it will cause cardiovascular damage and gastrointestinal problems, such as ulcers and irritated bowel syndrome, and decreased fertility. It can lead to accelerated aging and even premature death. This is what my pastor preached on; it was so good. Don't fear its facts, and its true: when we walk with God, we should not fear. This is why we shall repent and live in the name of God. People will talk about you as you grow, but just keep on praying and praising, and soon, you will see those people will watch you and laugh or will get up and do something about their lack for God. fearing will not help you at all. Fearing will keep you down and out. Get out of your fear, and you will feel good. Once you get over your fear of something, you will feel better about getting over something else that you are fearing, and it will get easier for you.

Start by eating healthy and going for a walk. I've had problems with my ankle hurting, but once I started eating better and working out, I started feeling better. Eating poorly will have an impact on you. If you want to change, you must change your eating and your lifestyle. Start drinking water and detox tea—always detox—it will help you clean yourself out. Your gut and your mind will clear. Remember: be a gardner. Every gardener knows that one of the secrets to heathy plants comes from cutting away the dead parts. When the leaves begin to wither and turn brown, that part of the plant has died and needs to be pruned. The dead parts can contaminate the healthy plant, and if the gardener refuses to prune, then the entire plant could die. In this passage, God is the gardener who must cut off the descendants of the wicked. He does this to protect the godly ones, the healthy part of the plant. He does this because He is God, and He wishes to preserve us forever. So, do not be afraid to cut people out of your life, so you can blossom.

A good prayer for this and your health is,

"Father, thank you for protecting me and preserving me. You have promised to cut off the wicked, so they will not prosper. I do not have to fear their descendants, because you have pruned them away. AMEN."

The Power of Not Weighing Yourself Down

Don't weigh yourself down. It's almost like driving a car with a bunch of weight in it, like taking cement and laying it down in the truck—it's going to drive funny—or swimming with rocks on your feet. Why do we do this to ourselves? I am going to tell you why. My favorite words were, "I can't afford it," or "I don't have time." Start telling yourself you can do it, and speak it into existence. "I will be able to afford it," "I will do it," not "I will try," nor, "I will see what I can do." You are basically saying "no" to yourself; don't be afraid of change. Give all that weight to God and let Him help you pray. He will change everything. Let the word of God fill you up.

Look on YouTube and listen to, "Fill Me Up/ Overflow"—it's a song I listen to.

The Power of Listening and for Others to Be Heard

Why do we go out to eat and stay on our phones the whole time? We don't communicate. Let's stop this; let's put our phones aside. Put your phones in the middle of the table, and whoever grabs their phone first will pay the bill, hahaha. God did not put ears on the side of our face to not listen. We can help save a life if we just listen without negative feedback. Don't judge, just help!

The Power of Thinking Big and Dreaming Big, is Up to You

Your dreams and your mindset are up to you, do what you want to do to help people or whatever your dream is. You can do it! Put your mind to the test, and you can do whatever you want. I've trusted in God, and look where it has gotten me. Don't fear, don't wake up in a bad mood, saying, "Well, today is ruined." No, no, no; think positive, and say, "Yes, today is going to be good day." Stay with that, even if you go outside to start your car and it will not start. Say, "Well, I have a car, and I just need a jump." You never know, that delay could have saved your life, and remember: change your ways. Cussing or cursing is a curse; let's try to use better words. This is what I am working on now. If you have a dream, don't be afraid to change for the better. Yes, I've had lots of jobs and moving from place to place, but that is why you start something you are passionate about and keep going. A job will help you along the way to fulfill your businesses. Making it is not cheap, but let me tell you, it's so rewarding, better than a job. Just over broke, don't live your life building someone else's dream. Build your own dream, it's not easy, but it is so fun. HEB has been a huge blessing and helping me but really i am taking the step to help myself in business

The Power of Praying

When I was growing up, I never went to church; I never really thought about going until I met Autumn, the same girl I moved to Texas with. She told me, "You need to go, and you need to seek a therapist." I said, "Okay." I believed her, and I did not think I was going to be dropping to my knees and praying. I have been looking at my Bible, and it says the meaning of worship. Worship refers to the honor and praise given in thought or deed to a person or thing. The Bible teaches that God, alone, is worthy of worship. I did not realize that I should be treating myself the same way and worship myself the way that God sees me. God loves us and wants us to be happy. I've seen people so angry and be freed by the power of God and His Word. My church has made me see that also being strong, courageous, and of not being afraid or discouraged to let out a roar like a lion and be free. It's such a beautiful thing.

When Autumn told me about her church, I wanted to go, and I did. I was falling in love with Athey Creek pastor bryan gave us the word and hes is the one that got me into the bible. I got baptized in the river by one of the pastors at athehy creek. I cried, I was so happy, I came out new and fresh when we moved to Texas. I did not know anyone, but when I met Krystal, she invited me to her church ascension city church pastor Bobby. When I met people at her church, they were so amazing. I overhauled someone's house and got to help with different stuff and serve. Overhauling vanasnas and anthonys home was so awesome; it brought joy to my heart. We took a negative situation and now, they can live in that home and be happy as i was putting my hands to that home i realised i felt the holy spirit move and i was exetited. Anthony and Vanessa are a married couple; they are so amazing, as are their kids. Anthony has his own auto mechanic shop, Flores Machine and Garage. It's so good he works there with his dad. When my car messed up, he was right there with me. I've been blessed by all the people who have helped me and bless all the people who have done me wrong. All of the people who have done me wrong have been a blessing, because we have to forgive them and keep moving forward.

Anthony and his wife, Vanessa, moved from Ascension City Church to a new church Xtheme harvest church with pastor Brian. I saw them and their kids grow more for God; it was a beautiful thing. I love Ascension Church and the people there; I just wanted more of God. When I got to Xtreme Harvest Church, I felt God move through my heart, and I fell to my knees, praying. It was the most beautiful thing; I believe God has put in my heart to do this business and take care of my animals. Being strong as believing in myself and knowing I can do this. God also told me to make my logo as a heart, so that I can touch everyone with my logo in love and purple is my favoriote color. If you look at it, springing scales, it has a big purple heart where i am the heart you you are the star. I did that for the love of the animals, and now I am starting a non-profit organization. I can't wait for that. I just have to do some paperwork, and by the time this book is done, my nonprofit will be.

The Power of Your Dream

What do you dream about, and how do you overcome it? My dream, as you already know, is to help adults understand the power of loving yourself, the power of healing, and forgiveness of your wrong doings and self-love.

My biggest dream is to help kids with disabilities and help them understand that these animals are not as bad as you think. Now, I live in a two-bed, one-bath apartment, but I am thankful for what I have. I want to open a warehouse for kids. The front will be the check in, and as they go in, it will be a huge bounce house, and as they enter, the parents can see them having fun. It will be like an obstacle course; it will be a lizard shape, and they will enter the mouth of the bounce house and slide down the tail. I want a nice area for the parents, so they can relax and drink my TLC detox tea while the kids are playing. I also would love to have a massage chair or one of those water massage chairs. Total relaxation for the parents. As the kids walk in through the bounce house, they can play, and when they are done inside the bounce house, they come out into a trampoline park. I was a gymnast, so I can do back flips. After that, I would love to have a couple of party rooms and the reptile sanctuary in the back.

I can't wait until things take off. I want some education toys for the kids, and if I do have TVs, they will be on the Discovery Channel or on Wishbone or magic school bus. I want to bring back the old school kids' shows. I am a sponsor for a kid in Uganda, and I want to travel to his home and provide education for the kids with the animals. That's my dream, and working at a JOB I will not have time for, but in God's time, it will come. It's already taking off. Later down the line, I will need a truck, so I can put my logo on it. I like big, lifted trucks, and to have all of this would make me cry. If your dream doesn't make you cry or work for free at it, then you need to dream bigger.

Right now, I am volunteering for Once in a Wild Zoo, and she's amazing. Her soon-to-be husband does the website and marketing. I love them, she's so good with her animals, and her parents are sweet. I also volunteer with her with the reptiles. Her dad is an amazing artist. I will be helping the YMCA and becoming a sponsor for them. I am so happy that I found my calling.

The Power of Knowing What You Are Worth

I know we all like to help people, but the most important thing is to help ourselves, so we can help other people. Knowing your worth is how people will treat you. If you think you are worth crap, then that's how you will be treated, but if you see yourself worth more, then by the power of God, people will run away from that. Then, you will see yourself worth more, tell yourself you are worth millions, and you will attract the right people. Start telling yourself, I am worth more than this. This is just temporary. Speak life into what you do, and speak into existence. Then, you will think positive and be more effective on your decisions and dreams. You make your dreams come alive by speaking them in existence like they're already happening. Take negative situations and turn them around, especially if people laugh at you. Take that, and let that add fuel to your fire as they laugh at you. Do it two times, as they don't believe in you. Believe in yourself and keep going. God will send you the right people to help you keep focused. There is nothing wrong with having more than one person cheering you on, but make sure you cheer yourself on and keep going. Tell yourself you are worth more than crap, believe in yourself, and certainly celebrate yourself and victory.

The Power of Finding a Good Church for Yourself

My parents did not go to church when I was growing up. I lived a sheltered life when I met Autumn at Safeway she was going to athey creek and she wated me to go so i did i never thought i was going to be able to add god to my life. when I moved to texas i saw some live streams of Vanessa's new church, so one day, I decided to go as i talked about it before i went and was saved by the power of gods love and the holy spirit. It was so good that I felt the Holy Spirit move though my heart. I dropped to my knees and prayed and cried, I have never felt anything like that before. I just cried and looked up and said, "Thank you, Jesus," such a good God thanks God yes God. If your pastor does not make you cry or change, I would look into something that will help you grow. Brian, my pastor now, is on fire. I love Xtreme Harvest and the people there are so Godly and humble. I loved Ascension, too, but it was time for me to move on and grow up. Let God touch your heart and be filled with the Holy Spirit. Don't be afraid to move with God. This will give you the power to understand what I am saying in this book. Open a Bible. This will give you the power to love yourself as you should, and will help you in situations to forgive. Forgive yourself of your sins, and it will move you in the power that you need to get through your day. You will see change in your heart and spirit. I am telling you that it is a beautiful thing, and God will take out negative people and put things in that are only for you and His kingdom. I love you all. Please take care of yourself and have fellowship. If you guys need anything, let me know. I have my Facebook, and I go live where I am. If you have any questions about snakes or lizards, I am here for you. Let God be there for you. Remember: God does not want you to try harder. He wants you to trust Him deeper. Stop trying; trying will lead to failure. Start trusting, and this will change everything in you. Thank you, God, I am happy I can share this with You.

Put God first, this is what I pray in the morning before I wake up. In the morning, before I open my eyes, I get out of my bed, get on my knees, and pray. Then, I look at this.

It's my life dedication to Christ.

Romans 12:1 Beseech you therefore, brethren, by the mercies of God that you present your bodies a living sacrifice holy and acceptable to God, which is your reasonable service.

Worship is not just a song. It is an expression of your love and appreciation for God.

God, today I dedicate my mind to You. I want to think on things that are good, right, pure, and excellent. Philippians 4:8

I want to take captive any thoughts that aren't from You 2 for 10:5 I want to remember your past faithfulness when I am tempted to doubt. Proverbs 3:5

Today, I dedicate my eyes to you. I want to see others the way you see them. I want to view my circumstances through the lens of hope and faith. I want to look at life as one who is confident that you are with me.

Today, I dedicate my ears to you. I want to hear your voice above all the others, clamoring for my attention, knowing that faith comes by hearing and hearing the world of God. Luke 18:36

I want to listen to you and to honor others by listening well to them. James 1:19

Today, I dedicate my mouth to you. I want my words to be life-giving. Proverbs 18:21

I want to speak honestly and sincerely. I want to think before I speak and say only what you say. I want to only put in my mouth what glorifies Your temple. 1 Corinthians 6:20

Today, I dedicate my heart to you. I want my heart to be pure and undivided. I want to master my emotions and not serve them. I want my dreams and desire to please you.

Today, I dedicate my hands to you. I want to work hard at whatever I put my hands to. I want to touch others in love and good will. I want my hands to be open for whatever you want to give me and willing to release anything you want me to surrender.

Today, I dedicate my feet to you. I want to go wherever you send me. I want to walk towards the messes, not run from them. I want to stand firmly upon the truth and not stumble.

Today I give my mind, body, and soul to glorify and honor, You, my savor and lord of my life. In Jesus, name Amen.

Remember, run, spring forward, and do not go back i actually ran and did a cartwheel and a backhand spring on stage in may look like a mess of flips but it does not have to.let God clear your mind and heal that was my speech and to get over fear God helped me to become a internatial best selling author and a keynote speaker and a reptile handler thank you jeasus

I want to encourage you; you may be tempted to turn your back on those who seem weak, but we should not. For example, a team will work to support its weakest member, so we should work to support those who are weak, because it is what we are called to do. So that Christ may be revealed when we help those who are weak. We should not do it for recognition of our own strength. We should help others as Christ helped us. We shall forgive and love.

Pray This

Dear God, when I am tempted to prove my own strength in light of someone else's weaknesses, help me to remember your sacrifice, o Lord, you deserve all the glory, not me. Forgive me for being prideful. Help me to guide those who need it, so that you may be glorified as I grow closer to you. Allow me to walk alongside younger believers and encourage them as well. In Jesus' name, amen.

I am here for you guys and I belive in you.
Stanitrarobinson@yahoo.com

springingscales.com
my business website

I am also on instagram

God bless you and I hope this helps you to love yourself

Special Thanks

ACKNOWLEDGEMENTS

Huge shout out to people who blessed me special thanks from my heart.

♥Brian Ayala the best Pastor at Xtreme Harvest Church thanks for being real true to God and his word don't stop much to you and your family Pastor Cija

♥B-raw podcast Sholonda Lonnie Mack

♥Be Michelle the branding coach

♥San Antonio Anthony

♥Daniel Gomez Enterprise and Mari Strong Foundation non-profit

♥coach les starting the morning off right with a cup of bible on clubhouse

♥Michael D. Bulter for publishing my books at Beyond Publishing

♥Sis Trica for understanding me I love you♥

♥Kevin Castillo podcast

♥Andria Odom for being so crafty

♥YMCA kids club

♥SA preparatory school Coach Devin

♥herbal life nutrition

♥Darline Romeo Lopez ♥the pink ring club ⟲

♥Regeline Gigi Sabbat

♥Clifton Simmons let's not make it awkward

♥TLC family

♥kissy Denise

♥Victorian black Swann inn

Thank you all God bless you guys

www.ingramcontent.com/pod-product-compliance
Lightning Source LLC
LaVergne TN
LVHW022002060526
838200LV00003B/64